This book belongs to:

Lindsay

Have a great senior year! I love you with all my !

Mommy :)

69468876R00068

Made in the USA
San Bernardino, CA
15 February 2018